The Way to the Zoo

The Way to the Zoo

Poems about Animals chosen by

David Jackson

Oxford University Press

Oxford Toronto Melbourne

Oxford University Press, Walton Street, Oxford OX2 6DP

Oxford   London   Glasgow
New York   Toronto   Melbourne   Auckland
Kuala Lumpur   Singapore   Hong Kong   Tokyo
Delhi   Bombay   Calcutta   Madras   Karachi
Nairobi   Dar es Salaam   Cape Town

and associate companies in
Beirut   Berlin   Ibadan   Mexico City   Nicosia

Selection, arrangement and editorial matter
© Oxford University Press 1983

Oxford is a trademark of Oxford University Press

First published 1983

ISBN 0 19 276045 9

British Library Cataloguing in Publication Data

The way to the Zoo
   1. English poetry   2. Animals—Juvenile poetry
   I. Title
   821'.008036   PR1195.A/

   ISBN 0-10-276045-9

Phototypeset by Tradespools Limited,
Frome, Somerset.

Printed and bound in Great Britain by
William Clowes Limited, Beccles and London

Contents

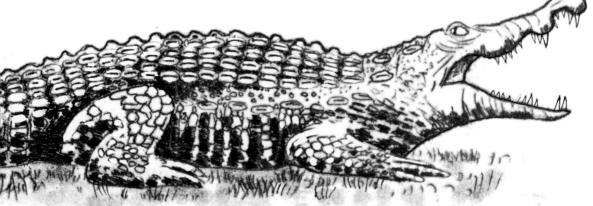

Small Creatures

The Wilderness

Imaginary Creatures

Water Creatures

The Way to the Zoo

That's the way to the zoo,
That's the way to the zoo,
The monkey house is nearly full
But there's room enough for you.

Children's street rhyme

Egg O egg
shape of mouth
saying O

not speaking
keeping your
secrets

O
little world
keeping life
warm and dumb

until *crack!*
and the world
begins

beak
pecks and wet
from within
squeaks
a chick

Keith Bosley

Birth

It lay there
A small brown oval.
It heaved out and
Bulged. A little hole
Appeared.
The shell around
Began to push back
Like minute tidal waves.
Cracks reached out like
Tentacles across the
Fragile surface.
They slowly widened
Like an earth splitting up.
More tidal waves
Swirl across the surface.
Pieces of shell fly out in
All directions as the hole
Widens.
The interior hurls
Itself at the air.

Rolled up in a
Bundle among
The wreckage of the
Shell lay a little heap of
Yellow.

Peter Alan Sirman

11

A Newly-born Calf

A newly-born calf
is like oven-baked bread
steaming under a cellophane cover.
The cow cuts
the shiny coat,
as a child would
lick a toffee,
with a tongue as pink as
the sole of a foot.
The calf sways on legs
filled with jelly and custard
instead of bone and marrow;
and it totters
to suck the teats
of its mother's udder.

Oswald Mtshali

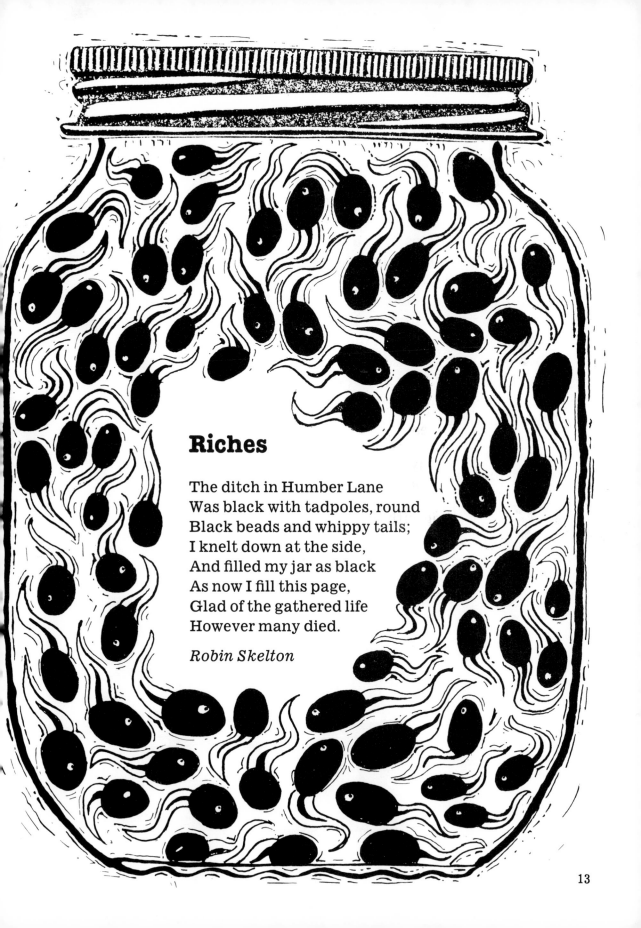

Riches

The ditch in Humber Lane
Was black with tadpoles, round
Black beads and whippy tails;
I knelt down at the side,
And filled my jar as black
As now I fill this page,
Glad of the gathered life
However many died.

Robin Skelton

Greedy Dog

This dog will eat anything.

Apple cores and bacon fat,
Milk you poured out for the cat.
He likes the string that ties the roast
And relishes hot buttered toast.
Hide your chocolates! He's a thief,
He'll even eat your handkerchief.
And if you don't like sudden shocks,
Carefully conceal your socks.
Leave some soup without a lid,
And you'll wish you never did.
When you think he must be full,
You find him gobbling bits of wool,
Orange peel or paper bags,
Dusters and old cleaning rags.

This dog will eat anything,
Except for mushrooms and cucumber.

Now what is wrong with those, I wonder?

James Hurley

14

I do not understand

I do not understand
ARF
How people
ARF
GROWL
BARK
Can walk around on two
ARF
Legs.
I see them in the park
BARK
And all around the town.
They walk around on just two legs
Without
BARK
Falling down!
ARF

Karla Kuskin

15

Better be kind to them now

A squirrel is digging up the bulbs
In half the time Dad took to bury them.

A small dog is playing football
With a mob of boys. He beats them all,
Scoring goals at both ends.
A kangaroo would kick the boys as well.

Birds are so smart they can drink milk
Without removing the bottle-top.

Cats stay clean, and never have to be
Carried screaming to the bathroom.
They don't get their heads stuck in railings,
They negotiate first with their whiskers.

The gecko walks on the ceiling, and
The cheetah can outrun the Royal Scot.
The lion cures his wounds by licking them,
And the guppy has fifty babies at a go.

The cicada plays the fiddle for hours on end,
And a man-size flea could jump over St Paul's.

If ever these beasts should get together
Then we are done for, children.
I don't much fancy myself as a python's pet,
But it might come to that.

D. J. Enright

16

Dog-Talk

Dogs love one another
in very doggy ways;
they don't say much
and they don't waste time,
as they chat with a bark or two.

They woof and snuffle,
in friendly talk when noses meet
and paws go up,
just to say 'how-do',
as they stop for a sniff or two.

Judith Thurman

I have this crazy problem

When I was young
about six years old
I wanted a dog.

I asked my mum and dad
to buy me a dog
but all the time
they would say no.

So from that day onwards
I started to steal dogs.
I would get a dog or two
a day.

Now I am twenty-five years old and
I have collected
about five hundred dogs.

Mohammed Khan

Who to pet and who not to

Go pet a kitten, pet a dog,
Go pet a worm for practice,
But don't go pet a porcupine —
You want to be a cactus?

X. J. Kennedy

A Guinea-pig

A furry animal,
An explorer,
A fast mover,
And a maker of holes.

He likes carrots,
He likes biscuits,
He likes chocolate,
And he ate Crispin.

Crispin was a flea.

Hugh Hodge

19

Our Hamster's Life

Our hamster's life:
there's not much
to it,
not much
to it.

He presses his pink nose
to the door of his cage
and decides for the fifty six
millionth time
that he can't get
through it.

Our hamster's life:
there's not much
to it,
not much
to it.

It's about the most boring
life in the world,
if he only
knew it.
He sleeps and he drinks and he eats.
He eats and he drinks and he sleeps.

He slinks and he dreeps.
He eats.

This process
he repeats.

Our hamster's life:
there's not much
to it,
not much
to it.

You'd think it would drive him bonkers,
going round and round on his wheel.
It's certainly driving me bonkers,

watching him
do it.

But he may be thinking:
'That boy's life,
there's not much
to it,
not much
to it:

watching a hamster go round on a wheel.
It's driving me bonkers if he only knew it,

watching him
watching me
do it.'

Kit Wright

Cat

My cat has got no name,
We simply call him Cat;
He doesn't seem to blame
Anyone for that.

For he is not like us
Who often, I'm afraid,
Kick up quite a fuss
If *our* names are mislaid.

As if, without a name,
We'd be no longer there
But like a tiny flame
Vanish in bright air.

My pet, he doesn't care
About such things as that:
Black buzz and golden star
Require no name but Cat.

Vernon Scannell

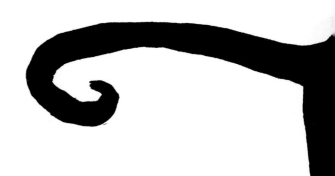

Stormy

what name could
better
explode from

a sleeping pup
but this
leaping

to his feet
Stormy!
Stormy!
Stormy!

William Carlos Williams

If you,

If you,
Like me,
Were made of fur
And sun warmed you,
Like me,
You'd purr.

Karla Kuskin

Disturbed, the cat
Lifts its belly
On to its back.

Modern Senryu

Cat purring

Cat
purring

four furry paws
walking

delicate-
ly
   between
flower stems
stalking

butter-
flies

Keith Bosley

Cat and the Weather

Cat takes a look at the weather.
Snow.
Puts a paw on the sill.
His perch is piled, is a pillow.

Shape of his pad appears.
Will it dig? No.
Not like sand.
Like his fur almost.

But licked, not liked.
Too cold.
Insects are flying, fainting down.
He'll try

to bat one against the pane.
They have no body and no buzz.
And now his feet are wet:
it's a puzzle.

Shakes each leg,
then shakes his skin
to get the white flies off.
Looks for his tail,

tells it to come on in
by the radiator.
World's turned queer
somehow. All white,

no smell. Well, here
inside it's still familiar.
He'll go to sleep until
it puts itself right.

May Swenson

Farmyard

Little hen
feathered and red
pecking round for scraps of bread.

Little goat
fierce and white
thinks his rope is much too tight.

Little calf
soft and shy
peeking out with one brown eye.

Little cat
black and lean
crouching so he won't be seen.

Little pig
muddy and stout
trying hard to wriggle out.

Gail Gregory

Old Horse

He's worked out
like a lead-mine, grey
dusty deserted,
lost for metal hammering metal,
clatter of feet and gear.

Head hung over a gate,
lower lip drooped
disconsolate,
he stands unmoving.
Then suddenly flings his mane
whipping a gauze of flies
that suck the juices
round suppurating eyes.

No one comes
to lead him to the stable, feed him oats
and polish his flanks to silver.
Lead-grey, weight
carried on three legs,
he sags with the sodden day
wrong side of the gate.

Phoebe Hesketh

Horse

The picnickers were sleeping when I,
deciding to be an enormous black horse not seen
in the corner of their field, strolled over.

They had a tartan rug, and a
thermos flask, and they had unwrapped
and eaten little triangles of processed

cheese, with tomatoes. They had been
playing cards among the thistles and
water-biscuits, and had fallen asleep

in the very hot sun. So I was a sudden, black
alarming shadow standing over them, though really
just inquisitive. When one of them heard the
    sound of my breath.

and woke, having dreamt of dragons, and
leapt up and shouted, *I* had to pretend to
be frightened of *them* and gallop away.

Alan Brownjohn

Mare

When the mare shows you
her yellow teeth, stuck
with clover and gnawed leaf,
you know they have combed
pastures of spiky grasses,
and tough thickets.

But when you offer her
a sweet, white lump
from the trembling plate
of your palm — she trots
to the gate, sniffs —
and takes it with velvet lips.

Judith Thurman

The Mules

In the world of mules
There are no rules.

Ogden Nash

The Slabbery Fingers

My fingers slide down the little calf's throat,
Its tongue is rough and pink,
It sucks and slurps
And nearly pulls my fingers off.

It slabbers like a baby
And makes my fingers sticky,
No matter how hard I pull
It just won't let me go.

At last I am free, and look at my fingers,
They are covered in little bubbles
And they nearly make me sick.
The calf puts out its head, but I'm away.

Fiona Davison

Cows

The cows that browse in pastures
Seem not at all surprised
That as they moo they mow the lawn
And their milk comes pasture-ized.

X. J. Kennedy

Hay in Winter

The bullocks trample at the gate,
The tractor rumbles near,
Fred on the trailer forks the hay,
Winter is hard this year.
The grass is poor,
The ground is hard
Under the hooves
Like stable yard.
They toss their horns and jostle round;
High-tasselled tails on bony rumps
See-saw and bound;
The crescent curve of scattered hay
Pulls down the heads,
A rustling, dark,
Suddenly-ordered curve of beasts
Tethered by hunger in an arc.

Leonard Clark

White Cat

I like to go to the stable after supper, —
Remembering fried potatoes and tarts of snow-apple jam —
And watch the men curry the horses,
And feed the pigs, and especially give the butting calves
    their milk.
When my father has finished milking he will say,
'Now Howard, you'll have to help me carry in these pails.
How will your mother be getting along
All this time without her little man?'
So we go in, and he carries them, but I help.
My father and I don't need the lanterns.
They hang on the wires up high back of the stalls
And we leave them for Ern and Dick.
It seems such a long way to the house in the dark,
But sometimes we talk, and always
There's the White Cat, that has been watching
While my father milked.
In the dark its gallop goes before like air,
Without any noise,
And it thinks we're awfully slow
Coming with the milk.

Raymond Knister

The Noises at Night

At night,
when my brothers and sister are asleep
I hear the mice scampering across the attic floor.
I think to myself
They will pull all the feathers off
my daddy's stuffed birds.

Dominick Vallely

Anne and the Field-Mouse

We found a mouse in the chalk quarry today
In a circle of stones and empty oil drums
By the fag ends of a fire. There had been
A picnic there; he must have been after the crumbs.

Jane saw him first, a flicker of brown fur
In and out of the charred wood and chalk-white.
I saw him last, but not till we'd turned up
Every stone and surprised him into flight.

Though not far — little zigzag spurts from stone
To stone. Once, as he lurked in his hiding place,
I saw his beady eyes uplifted to mine.
I'd never seen such terror in so small a face.

I watched, amazed and guilty. Beside us suddenly
A heavy pheasant whirred up from the ground,
Scaring us all, and, before we knew it, the mouse
Had broken cover, skimming away without sound,

Melting into the nettles. We didn't go
Till I'd chalked in capitals on a rusty can:
THERE'S A MOUSE IN THOSE NETTLES. LEAVE
HIM ALONE. NOVEMBER 15th. ANNE.

Ian Serraillier

The Meadow Mouse

In a shoe box stuffed in an old nylon stocking
Sleeps the baby mouse I found in the meadow,
Where he trembled and shook beneath a stick
Till I caught him up by the tail and brought him in,
Cradled in my hand,
A little quaker, the whole body of him trembling,
His absurd whiskers sticking out like a cartoon-mouse,
His feet like small leaves,
Little lizard-feet,
Whitish and spread wide when he tried to struggle away,
Wriggling like a miniscule puppy.

Now he's eaten his three kinds of cheese and drunk from
    his bottle-cap watering-trough —
So much he just lies in one corner,
His tail curled under him, his belly big
As his head; his bat-like ears
Twitching, tilting toward the least sound.

Do I imagine he no longer trembles
When I come close to him?
He seems no longer to tremble.

But this morning the shoe-box house on the back porch is
    empty.
Where has he gone, my meadow mouse,
My thumb of a child that nuzzled in my palm? —
To run under the hawk's wing,
Under the eye of the great owl watching from the elm-tree,
To live by courtesy of the shrike, the snake, the tom-cat.

I think of the nestling fallen into the deep grass,
The turtle gasping in the dusty rubble of the highway,
The paralytic stunned in the tub, and the water rising, —
All things innocent, hapless, forsaken.

Theodore Roethke

The Ladybird

Tiniest of turtles
Your shining back
Is a shell of orange
With spots of black.

How trustingly you walk
Across this land
Of hairgrass and hollows
That is my hand.

Clive Sansom

Small, smaller

I thought that I knew all there was to know
Of being small, until I saw once, black against the snow,
A shrew, trapped in my footprint, jump and fall
And jump again and fall, the hole too deep, the walls too tall.

Russell Hoban

The Worm

Don't ask me how he managed
to corkscrew his way
through the King Street Pavement,
I'll leave that to you.

All I know is
there he was,
circling, uncoiling
his shining three inches,
wiggling all ten toes
as the warm rain fell
in that dark morning street
of early April.

Raymond Souster

The worm thinks it strange and foolish
    that man does not eat his books.

Rabindranath Tagore

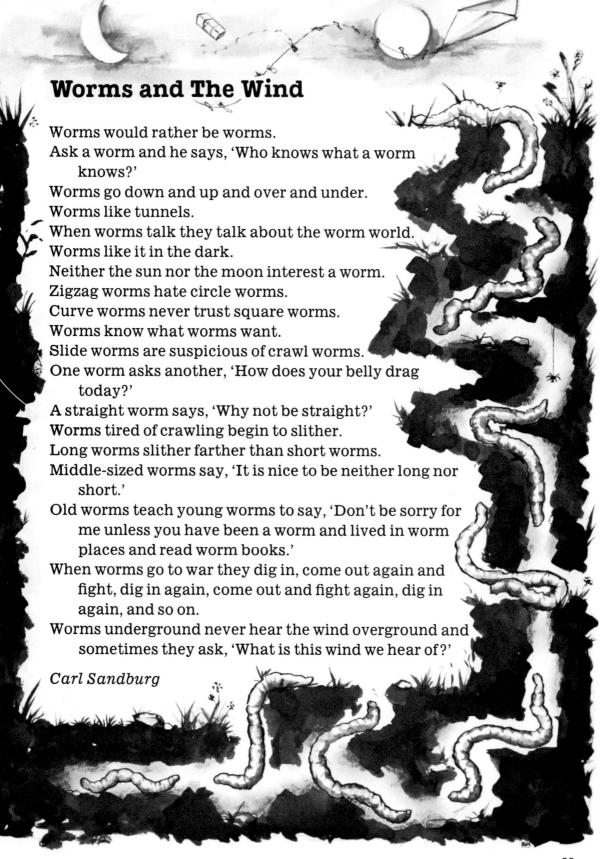

Worms and The Wind

Worms would rather be worms.
Ask a worm and he says, 'Who knows what a worm
    knows?'
Worms go down and up and over and under.
Worms like tunnels.
When worms talk they talk about the worm world.
Worms like it in the dark.
Neither the sun nor the moon interest a worm.
Zigzag worms hate circle worms.
Curve worms never trust square worms.
Worms know what worms want.
Slide worms are suspicious of crawl worms.
One worm asks another, 'How does your belly drag
    today?'
A straight worm says, 'Why not be straight?'
Worms tired of crawling begin to slither.
Long worms slither farther than short worms.
Middle-sized worms say, 'It is nice to be neither long nor
    short.'
Old worms teach young worms to say, 'Don't be sorry for
    me unless you have been a worm and lived in worm
    places and read worm books.'
When worms go to war they dig in, come out again and
    fight, dig in again, come out and fight again, dig in
    again, and so on.
Worms underground never hear the wind overground and
    sometimes they ask, 'What is this wind we hear of?'

Carl Sandburg

Catching Butterflies

The daren't breathe steps
across a field of cow-clap and thistle.
The navy mac held up and out,
poised for the settling pause
on ragwort, nettle.

The wings open, close
open, close.
The air waits, listens.

Then the dark-blue rush and fall.

There's greyish dust on your mac sleeve.

David Jackson

The Butterfly

I always think the butterfly
Looks best against a clear blue sky;
I do not think he looks so good
Pinned down within a box of wood.

Author unknown

a mayfly
struggles down the stream
one wing flapping dry

John Wills

The Honeypot

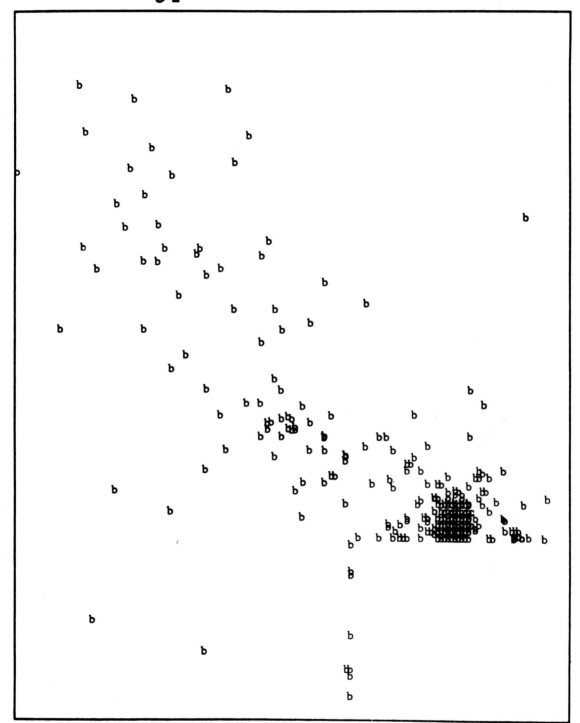

Alan Riddell

A wasp in a wasp-trap talks

I am a wasp.
I am stuck in a sticky jar.
I used to fly in the wind
buzz my wings in the sun
and hover in sweet places

but I am stuck in a sticky jar.

Up I fly
and my wings hit a tin lid
my hard yellow head knocks it
so down I glide for a flicker of a second
    and my legs, my body
are in sweet water where there is no breath
    to breathe.

I used to soar and swoop.
I used to circle round and round
and settle on sweet things

but I am stuck in a sticky jar.

Above me the heat of the sun
pours through holes in the tin.
I buzz and crawl to them.
Isn't that the way I came in?
—but nearly there, my feelers
    hit tin.
The ragged cut edge of tin.
And who am I to dare to drag this weak waist
across that edge?

Beneath me, all about me,
is the smell of crushed strawberry.
It doesn't grow stronger if I buzz nearer.

It doesn't grow weak if I hover or move.
It's strong everywhere in smell
and nowhere to be found.

I used to *find* crushed strawberries —
or maybe melting chocolate, the hearts
    of fat plums.
I used to cut my way to the syrup
    of bruised bananas
in the gutters of the market.
I used to linger on the rims of glasses and bottles
to nibble at the crystals of lemonade, cherryade
and old orange pop.

All around me now
other wasps, even a bee and a blue-bottle
buzz up buzz down
and we're all swerving to miss each other's wings.

I turn back.
One is at my foot.
I twist to dodge him
but he is at my neck.
I snip at his scales —
he twists, a hairsbreadth from my eye.
A sting sticks, waves to find
a soft spot to get in.
I cut back, take off
and my wing is flying in the sweet water
dragging me down.

I use my legs and run up over the backs
of wasps floating where water and glass meet.
They sink. I sink.
And the buzz in the sweet smell of the air
goes on and on.
There is heat in the sun through the holes
in the lid of the tin.

The heat pours in.
Up above me, my eyes shadowy with the sugar
see a hole for the heat.

Into it come the eyes, the feelers, the jaws,
the head, the legs, the chest, the —

Those of us in here could say:
Go back.

But those of us in here who could say
are no more than black and yellow scum,
dead froth bobbing on the water.

In through the hole comes the chest,
the wings, the waist, the body and the sting.

Too late,
you silly, sugar-sniffing, soft nibbling,
    sweet-sucker.
That's the end.

Michael Rosen

During a downpour,
the frog's eyes
— open

Virginia Brady Young

Old dark sleepy pool ...
Quick unexpected frog
Goes plop! Watersplash!

Matsuo Bashō
Translated by *Peter Beilenson*

The Frog's Lament

'I can't bite
like a dog,'
said the bright
green frog.

'I can't nip,
I can't squirt,
I can't grip,
I can't hurt.

'All I can do
is hop and hide
when enemies come
from far and wide.

'I can't scratch
like a cat.
I'm no match
for a rat.

'I can't stab,
I can't snare,
I can't grab,
I can't scare.

'All I can do
my whole life through
is hop,' said the frog,
'and hide from view.'

And that's
what I saw him
up and do.

Judith Thurman

The Frog

Slimy, greasy, Olympic jumper,
Leaping, springing, flying through the air.

No numbered T-shirt on his back,
To leap the hurdles on the track,
No crowd to watch his brilliant spring.
Just other frogs who do the same thing.

Sheelagh Carville

The World of the
Wash Basin Spider

The Wash Basin Spider's life is spent
In a slippery white enamel world
Of scented landmarks:
Shaving-brush shade tree,
Safety razor cannon,
Toothpaste tube and toothbrush road-blocks,
Stonehenge bars of soap,
One for the sunrise basin
And one for the Druidic bath.

Then there are the underground horrors,
Coming round the bend:
Knocking noises,
Tappet-knocks,
Half-hearted gushes,
Vicious spurts.

But the Spider's miniature Atlantic,
Rubber plugged, hot or cold,
Is as final as rain: with the Sargasso
Waiting down the drain.

Andrew Salkey

Poem to Spiders

The web
you so intricately
wove
between the cracked wall
and the screen
long ago,
where old insects hang
patiently
dying in wait for you

Rachel Fewster

The Spider

I'm told that the spider
Has coiled up inside her
Enough silky material
To spin an aerial
One-way track
to the moon and back;
Whilst I
Cannot even catch a fly.

Author unknown

The Gnat Bloated with Blood and Pride

The gnat flew round the jungle
Boasting of its powers,
It landed on a lion's back
And sucked lion-blood for hours.

The lion itched and with its claws
Tried to scratch the insect off.
'What's this?' cried the puffed-up gnat,
'A fight unto the death?'

'I'm strong as any lion,
As any tiger, as any beast!
I'm a ferocious thing
And on them all I feast!'

Bleeding from its scratching
The lion called off the fight.
'I concede,' said the itching creature,
'That you are probably right.'

Puffed up with blood and pride
The stupid gnat flew off,
It landed in a spider's web
And cried before its death:

'How inglorious to be killed by a spider!
It is such an insignificant thing.
To think I have come to this!
I, who fought once with a king!'

Brian Patten

The Termite

Some primal termite knocked on wood
And tasted it, and found it good,
And that is why your Cousin May
Fell through the parlour floor today.

Ogden Nash

Caterpillar

C rawls like a miniature ocean,
A rriving at an unknown destination,
T enderly feels around a leaf,
E very contact is brief, as if entering a naked flame.
R epeatedly moves its short legs,
P urposefully arches then straightens,
I gnorant of the prodding hand,
L eans, and falls to land upon a leaf below.
L azy, yet possessing a delightful beauty,
A drift in a world of dizziness —
R ed stripes like bloodstained gashes on its back.

Mark Nathan

Honeybees are very tricky—
Honey doesn't make them sticky.

Russell Hoban

I Did Not Touch Him

On the way to school David and I spied a millipede, almost
    under my feet.
I was counting worms all the way down the road.
We had counted two hundred and fifteen by the time we
    saw the millipede.
He was a pale yellow, with little black feet.
I did not touch him but left him on his way
And made sure I didn't crush him.
Some creatures I crush without bothering
But not this one.
I hadn't seen one before.
I turned back and saw him trying to climb a rain-slithery
    fence,
But all his legs didn't help him,
And he dropped back to the path,
Feet-in-the-air,
Helpless.

Stuart Wilson

A Visitor

We had an unexpected
Visitor today,
She came in on the silver-beet
And was nearly washed away.

We found her struggling in the sink
And when her wings were dry,
Ladybird, quick as a wink,
Flew off into the sky.

Joan M. Shilton

In the Bush

In the bush
you might see
koalas dozing in a tree.
In the bush
you might hear
kangaroos thumping
very near,
lizards scuttling
through dry grass,
noisy parrots
flying past.
In the bush
tread with care —
you never know
what's hiding there!

Anne Le Roy

54

The Kangaroo

Old Jumpety-Bumpety-Hop-and-Go-One
Was lying asleep on his side in the sun.
This old Kangaroo, he was whisking the flies
(With his long glossy tail) from his ears and his eyes.
Jumpety-Bumpety-Hop-and-Go-One
Was lying asleep on his side in the sun,
Jumpety-Bumpety-Hop!

Author unknown

Leopard

I am one
of the great cats,
the spotted one

— a particular one:
a leopard run
away from a

team of leopards
in a circus.
Will they

notice me
roaming the
dark gardens like

a prowling leopard
in a dream,
buying sandwiches

at coffee-stalls,
travelling on
buses half-fare,

sitting in the
cinema when
the lights go up,

standing very still
among the
stuffed animals when

they come after me,
running with
their nets through

the galleries of the
City
Museum?

Alan Brownjohn

Boa Constrictor

Oh, I'm being eaten
By a boa constrictor,
A boa constrictor,
A boa constrictor,
I'm being eaten by a boa constrictor,
And I don't like it — one bit.
Well, what do you know?
It's nibblin' my toe.
Oh, gee,
It's up to my knee.
Oh my,
It's up to my thigh.
Oh, fiddle,
It's up to my middle.
Oh, heck,
It's up to my neck.
Oh, dread,
It's upmmmmmmmmmmmfffffffffff. . .

Shel Silverstein

Cheetah

A cheetah has metal girder teeth
it goes hurling down through the jungle
throwing out its fear

Darren Coyles

Puma

Within the Puma's golden head
    burn Jungle, flames and paradises.
And all who look into his red
and fiery eye by fury fed
    the Puma paralyses.

The Sun, the Orchid and the Snake
    like demons of the Bible
rage in his brow. The earthquake
and the volcanic mountain shake
    and tremble in his eyeball.

George Barker

Hyena

I am waiting for you.
I have been travelling all morning through the bush
and not eaten.
I am lying at the edge of the bush
on a dusty path that leads from the burnt-out kraal.
I am panting, it is midday, I found no water-hole.
I am very fierce without food and although my eyes
are screwed to slits against the sun
you must believe that I am prepared to spring.

What do you think of me?
I have a rough coat like Africa.
I am crafty with dark spots
like the bush-tufted plains of Africa.
I sprawl as a shaggy bundle of gathered energy
like Africa sprawling in its waters.
I trot, I lope, I slaver, I am a ranger.
I hunch my shoulders. I eat the dead.

Do you like my song?
When the moon pours hard and cold on the veldt
I sing, and I am the slave of darkness.
Over the stone walls and the mud walls and the
    ruined places
and the owls, the moonlight falls.
I sniff a broken drum. I bristle. My pelt is silver.
I howl my song to the moon — up it goes.
Would you meet me there in the waste places?

It is said I am a good match
for a dead lion. I put my muzzle
at his golden flanks, and tear. He
is my golden supper, but my tastes are easy.
I have a crowd of fangs, and I use them.
Oh and my tongue — do you like me
when it comes lolling out over my jaw
very long, and I am laughing?
I am not laughing.
But I am not snarling either, only
panting in the sun, showing you
what I grip
carrion with.

I am waiting
for the foot to slide,
for the heart to seize,
for the leaping sinews to go slack,
for the fight to the death to be fought to the death,
for a glazing eye and the rumour of blood.
I am crouching in my dry shadows
till you are ready for me.
My place is to pick you clean
and leave your bones to the wind.

Edwin Morgan

The Snake Song

Neither legs nor arms have I
But I crawl on my belly
And I have
Venom, venom, venom!

Neither horns nor hoofs have I
But I spit with my tongue
And I have
Venom, venom, venom!

Neither bows nor guns have I
But I flash fast with my tongue
And I have
Venom, venom, venom!

Neither radar nor missiles have I
But I stare with my eyes
And I have
Venom, venom, venom!

John Mbiti

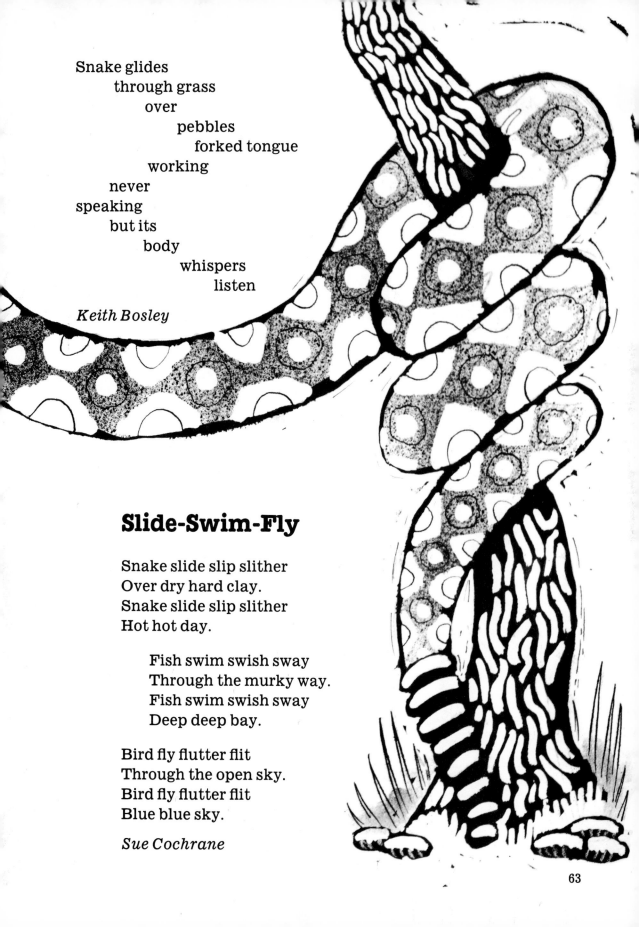

Snake glides
    through grass
       over
           pebbles
             forked tongue
       working
   never
speaking
   but its
       body
          whispers
            listen

Keith Bosley

Slide-Swim-Fly

Snake slide slip slither
Over dry hard clay.
Snake slide slip slither
Hot hot day.

   Fish swim swish sway
   Through the murky way.
   Fish swim swish sway
   Deep deep bay.

Bird fly flutter flit
Through the open sky.
Bird fly flutter flit
Blue blue sky.

Sue Cochrane

Eletelephony

Once there was an elephant,
Who tried to use the telephant—
No! no! I mean an elephone
Who tried to use the telephone—
(Dear me! I am not certain quite
That even now I've got it right.)

Howe'er it was, he got his trunk
Entangled in the telephunk;
The more he tried to get it free,
The louder buzzed the telephee—
(I fear I'd better drop the song
Of elephop and telephong!)

Laura E. Richards

Elephants Plodding

Plod! Plod!
And what ages of time
the worn arches of their spines support!

D. H. Lawrence

Buffalo Country

Out where the grey streams glide,
Sullen and deep and slow,
And the alligators slide
From the mud to the depths below
Or drift on the stream like a floating death,
Where the fever comes on the south wind's breath,
There is the buffalo.

Out on the big lagoons,
Where the Regia lilies float,
And the Nankeen heron croons
With a deep ill-omened note,
In the ooze and the mud of the swamps below
Lazily wallows the buffalo,
Buried to nose and throat.

From the hunter's gun he hides
In the jungles dark and damp,
Where the slinking dingo glides
And the flying foxes camp,
Hanging like myriad fiends in line
Where the trailing creepers twist and twine
And the sun is a sluggish lamp.

On the edge of the rolling plains
Where the coarse cane grasses swell,
Lush with the tropic rains
In the noon-tide's drowsy spell,
Slowly the buffalo grazes through
Where the brolgas dance, and the jabiru
Stands like a sentinel.

All that the world can know
Of the wild and the weird is here,
Where the black men come and go
With their boomerang and spear,
And the wild duck darken the evening sky
As they fly to their nests in the reedbeds high
When the tropic night is near.

A. B. Paterson

Mosquito

Mozzie

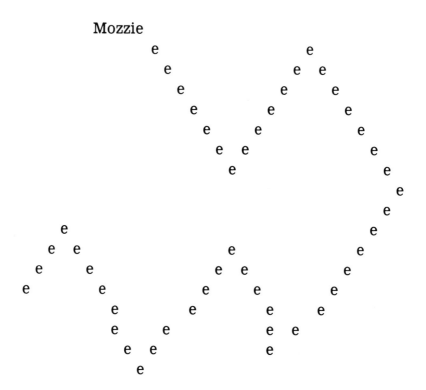

Marie Zbierski

The Zebra

The zebra is undoubtedly
a source of some confusion,
his alternating stripes present
an optical illusion.

Observing them is difficult,
one quickly loses track
of whether they are black on white
or rather, white on black.

Jack Prelutsky

Bear

Do not interfere with me;
I like to mind my own business.
If you hunt me down,
I shall outwit you, guns and all,
confuse you with false trails,
wait, affronted, in ambush,
until you pass by, then
charge with my 1500 fat pounds,
muscle and gold-brown fur,
red jaws ready to tear.
I am strong as rocks in Alaska.

Can send you flying with a blow,
senseless, from hammer claw,
pick up a whole deer,
carry secretly away, quiet as mouse,
through forest undergrowth,
shuffling my six-foot length along,
muzzle to printed ground,
swinging from side to side,
plenty of time in the world.

Keep away your dogs, too,
can crush them to pulp
between forepaws and ribs.
I am nasty when roused.

But do not see well,
eyes weak, too small,
can smell you out, though,
coarse scent on the wind,
or honey lodged in tree.
Am a fine climber,
balance better than acrobat,
on branches that take my weight;
sure head for heights,

not scared of mountain ledge;
a powerful swimmer,
lakes are all mine in summer,
loll silly in the sun.

I enjoy my own company,
am no great traveller,
but know the best places for roots,
sweet berries, grubs in old logs.
I live for green corn fields,
grapes at wine harvest,
very greedy for young salmon
silvering the July creeks,
will stuff myself with them,
chewing only the best bits.
I like a good joke.

And when the weather turns,
hills whiten with first flakes,
find some cave, hole in the ground,
block up entrance with trees,
any old rubbish, curl up,
caught in the season's sleep,
whatever winds may howl,
snow drift in the crevices,
drowse the long winter away,
getting leaner and leaner.

The cubs are born then;
she keeps them from me.
I do not mind, am too tired
to bother with them,
toothless and blind,
naked in the warm den.
She licks them one by one,
later will cuff them hard,
make them obey.

When icicles break,
I move off across the slopes
my father padded on,
thin as starved stoat,
thinking of redskin braves.
They worshipped all bears once,
begged their pardon, wept
when it came to the knife
and skin for the back.

I yawn away time.
A new sun shines,
rivers and woodlands call,
beetles and marmots creep out,
bees are at work for me.

Leonard Clark

The Small Brown Bear

The small brown bear
fishes
with stony paws

eating ice salmon
all waterfall slippery
till his teeth ache.

Michael Baldwin

Gorilla

Hairy arms, egg-shaped head;
Fierce appearance, but a gentle heart.
His shifty old eyes slide intelligently,
Searching the terrain.
As he eats his lower jaw rotates,
With a munch and a crunch he consumes his food.

His massive muscular body crouches tightly on the ground.
Heavily, clumsily, he swings through the trees,
He drops to the ground;
His arms are crutches — his body sways between them.
His legs are lazy and rarely used.

He scrambles behind wild bushes,
Then rustles,
Then, with a crash, he's gone.

Class 4S

Wilderness

There is a wolf in me . . . fangs pointed
for tearing gashes . . . a red tongue for
raw meat . . . and the hot lapping of
blood. I keep this wolf because the
wilderness gave it to me and the
wilderness will not let it go.

There is a fox in me . . . a silver-gray fox
. . . I sniff and guess . . . I pick things
out of the wind and air . . . I nose in
the dark night and take sleepers and
eat them and hide the feathers . . . I
circle and loop and double-cross.

There is a hog in me . . . a snout and a
belly . . . a machinery for eating and
grunting . . . a machinery for sleeping
satisfied in the sun — I got this too
from the wilderness and the
wilderness will not let it go.

There is a fish in me . . . I know I came
from salt-blue water-gates . . . I
scurried with shoals of herring . . . I
blew waterspouts with porpoises . . .
before land was . . . before the water
went down . . . before Noah . . . before
the first chapter of Genesis.

There is a baboon in me . . . clambering-
clawed . . . dog-faced . . . yawping a
galoot's hunger . . . hairy under the
armpits . . . here are the hawk-eyed
hankering men . . . here are the
blonde and blue-eyed women . . . here
they hide curled asleep waiting . . .
ready to snarl and kill . . . ready to
sing and give milk . . . waiting — I
keep the baboon because the
wilderness says so.

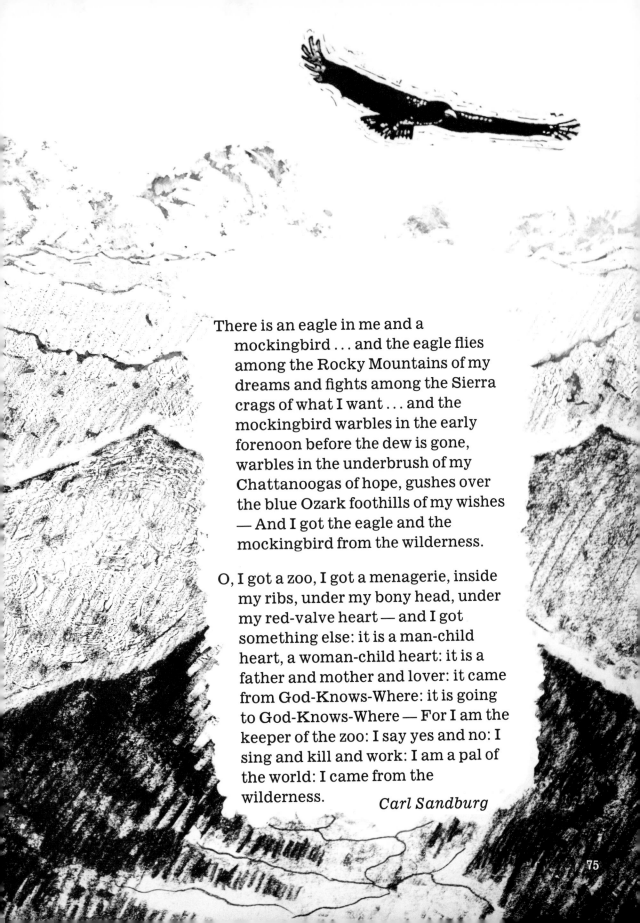

There is an eagle in me and a
    mockingbird ... and the eagle flies
    among the Rocky Mountains of my
    dreams and fights among the Sierra
    crags of what I want ... and the
    mockingbird warbles in the early
    forenoon before the dew is gone,
    warbles in the underbrush of my
    Chattanoogas of hope, gushes over
    the blue Ozark foothills of my wishes
    — And I got the eagle and the
    mockingbird from the wilderness.

O, I got a zoo, I got a menagerie, inside
    my ribs, under my bony head, under
    my red-valve heart — and I got
    something else: it is a man-child
    heart, a woman-child heart: it is a
    father and mother and lover: it came
    from God-Knows-Where: it is going
    to God-Knows-Where — For I am the
    keeper of the zoo: I say yes and no: I
    sing and kill and work: I am a pal of
    the world: I came from the
    wilderness.

Carl Sandburg

The Crocodile's Toothache

The Crocodile
Went to the dentist
And sat down in the chair,
And the dentist said, 'Now tell me, sir,
Why does it hurt and where?'
And the Crocodile said, 'I'll tell you the truth,
I have a terrible ache in my tooth,'
And he opened his jaws so wide, so wide,
That the dentist, he climbed right inside,
And the dentist laughed, 'Oh isn't this fun?'
As he pulled the teeth out, one by one.
And the Crocodile cried, 'You're hurting me so!
Please put down your pliers and let me go.'
But the dentist just laughed with a Ho Ho Ho,
And he said, 'I still have twelve to go —
Oops, that's the wrong one, I confess,
But what's one crocodile's tooth, more or less?'
Then suddenly, the jaws went SNAP,
And the dentist was gone, right off the map,
And where he went one could only guess . . .
To North or South or East or West . . .
He left no forwarding address.
But what's one dentist, more or less?

Shel Silverstein

Giraffe

Standing there on the ground
Making not a single sound
Your head up in the air
What's the weather like up there?

Emma O'Brien

Giraffe

At the zoo I saw: A long-necked, velvety Giraffe
Whose small head, high above the strawy, zooy smells
Seemed to be dreaming.
Was she dreaming of African jungles and African plains
That she would never see again?

Carson McCullers

77

The Thought-Fox

I imagine this midnight moment's forest:
Something else is alive
Beside the clock's loneliness
And this blank page where my fingers move.

Through the window I see no star:
Something more near
Though deeper within darkness
Is entering the loneliness:

Cold, delicately as the dark snow,
A fox's nose touches twig, leaf;
Two eyes serve a movement, that now
And again now, and now, and now

Sets neat prints into the snow
Between trees, and warily a lame
Shadow lags by stump and in hollow
Of a body that is bold to come

Across clearings, an eye,
A widening deepening greenness,
Brilliantly, concentratedly,
Coming about its own business

Till, with a sudden sharp hot stink of fox
It enters the dark hole of the head.
The window is starless still; the clock ticks,
The page is printed.

Ted Hughes

Yeti, The Abominable Snowman

High in the Himalayan west, between Kanchenjunga and Everest
the Abominable Yeti sleeps within its icy nest,
    and the mountain climbers know
    the one footprint in the snow
(which falls every morning like divine confetti)
    is the largest, not the least
    indication of this Beast,
the Abominable Snowman, the One and Only Yeti.

When he bivouacks at night on the Himalayan height
with the iceface glaring bright and the Moon an eerie white,
    the mountain climber hears
    the sad howl assail his ears
of the solitary Yeti in the Himalayan night.
    Restless and afraid and sweaty
    all alone the only Yeti
trembles in his icy nest of sheer loneliness and fright.

Yes, the Yeti weeps all day as, high among the Himalayas,
a New Zealander, two Sherpas and, I think, two native Mayas
    seek out its icy nest
    on the heights of Everest
while the Yeti kneels and trembles at its prayers.
    It's not praying for its life:
    it is praying for a wife,
for even Yetis should exist in pairs.

George Barker

The Worst

When singing songs of scariness.
Of bloodiness and hairyness,
I feel obligated at this moment to remind you
Of the most ferocious beast of all:
Three thousand pounds and nine feet tall —
The Glurpy Slurpy Skakagrall —
Who's standing right behind you.

Shel Silverstein

Dragon Poem

He comes in the night, killing all greenery,
with his spikey tail and rough scabby skin
killing all the humans and spitting the bones in the bin.

Frances Edwards

The Dinosaur

I sit in class
And imagine
The gates fall
And in comes a dinosaur.
I get on its back
And it carries me away.
It eats the teachers.
I escape from Colditz school.
I arrive in the jungle.
I travel to the Argentine.
I sit on the dinosaur's head
And look into the stadium.
Out come the Scotland team —
The dinosaur eats the Dutch team,
Then back home.
The dinosaur makes a submarine,
We both get in
And go home.
I get nudged
And the teacher tells me
To get on with my work.

Stewart Lackie

Monkey

I am easily
a monkey.
When the
front door
slams, I have
left the back
door open.
When a
teacup
spills on some
uncle's new
trousers, I
have pushed
it.
When the
curtains hang
down loose, I
have
unhooked them.

When
the key
or the scissors
or the string
is missing
I have
hidden them.
I am a
nuisance on
most holidays,
disrupting
adults'
intentions.
I will not ever
sit still in one
seat in the
car.

Alan Brownjohn

Word Owl

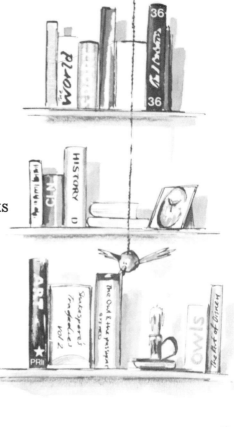

Never get up,
Shunning the cold,
Huddled in feathered fluff
Word Owl grows old.

Never get up,
Always in bed,
Flicking through all his books
Still to be read.

Never get up,
Snugged up and furred
This owl reads all the time
Speaks not a word.

Never get up,
Give him a shout;
Ask him why all these words
Never get out.

Fred Palmer

Nessie

No, it is not an elephant or any such grasshopper.
It's shaped like a pop bottle with two huge eyes in the
    stopper.

But vast as a gasometer, unmanageably vast,
With wing-things like a whale for flying underwater fast.

It's me, me, me, the Monster of the Loch!
Would God I were a proper kind, a hippopot or croc!

Mislaid by the ages, I gloom here in the dark.
When I should be ruling Scotland from a throne in
    Regent's Park!

Once I was nobility — Diplodocus ruled the Isles!
Polyptychod came courting with his stunning ten-foot
    smiles.

Macroplat swore he'd carry me off before I was much older.
All his buddy-boys were by, grinning over his shoulder —

Leptoclid, Cryptocleidus, Triclid and Ichthyosteg —
Upstart Sauropterygs! But I took him down a peg —

I had a long bath in the Loch and waiting till I'd finished
He yawned himself to a fossil and his gang likewise
    diminished.

But now I can't come up for air without a load of trippers
Yelling: 'Look at the neck on it, and look at its hedge-
    clippers!
Oh no, that's its mouth.' Then I can't decently dive
Without them sighing: 'Imagine! If *that* thing were alive!'

Why, we'd simply have to decamp, to Canada, and at the
    double!
It was luckily only a log, or the Loch-bed having a bubble.

It was something it was nothing why whatever could it be
The ballooning hideosity we thought we seemed to see?'

Because I am so ugly that it's just incredible!
The biggest bag of haggis Scotland cannot swallow or sell!

Me, me, me, the Monster of the Loch!
Scotland's ugliest daughter, seven tons of poppycock!

Living here in my black mud bed the life of a snittery
    newty.
And never a zoologist a-swooning for my beauty!

O where's the bonnie laddie, so bold and so free,
Will drum me up to London and proclaim my pedigree?

Ted Hughes

85

Elephantelope

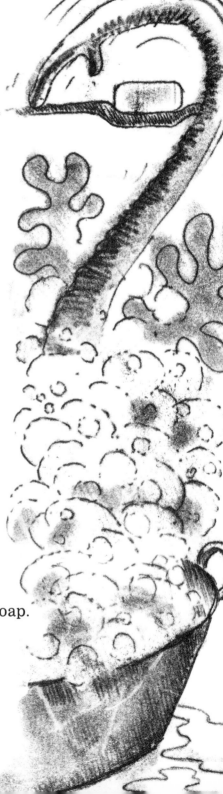

Poor old Elephantelope,
   he's looking still for that lost soap:
if he's sometimes cross or fretful
   it's because he's so forgetful:
forty times each livelong day
   he puts that precious soap away,
forty times each day to find
   that out of sight is out of mind.
'Where is it, that elusive cake?
   Where can it be, for goodness' sake?
Could I have left it in the tub,
   when I was having my morning rub?
Or in the soap-dish? or the sink?
   O dear, I simply cannot think!
Where did I put it? What did I do?
   Or was it yesterday, and you,
that had the bath, and lost the soap,
   and not old Elephantelope???
In the cupboard did I lock it?
   Or in my hind-leg trouser pocket?
Or is it swallowed down, and sunk,
   in my one and only trunk?
Perhaps I should buy soap in dozens,
   a cake with all its aunts and cousins,
for bathroom, kitchen, bedroom, hall —
   but then, good grief, I'd lose them all!
Or better still if I bought none,
   for then I could not lose a one! ...
If I could only, only find it,
   it's sad to be so absent-minded!'
And off he goes, his only hope
   (he says) that while there's life there's soap.

Conrad Aiken

86

The Bogus-Boo

The Bogus-boo
Is a creature who
Comes out at night — and why?
He likes the air;
He likes to scare
The nervous passer-by.

Out from the park
At dead of dark
He comes with huffling pad.
If, when alone,
You hear his moan,
'Tis like to drive you mad.

He has two wings,
Pathetic things,
With which he cannot fly.
His tusks look fierce,
Yet could not pierce
The merest butterfly.

He has six ears,
But what he hears
Is very faint and small;
And with the claws
On his eight paws
He cannot scratch at all.

He looks so wise
With his owl-eyes,
His aspect grim and ghoulish;
But truth to tell,
He sees not well
And is distinctly foolish.

This Bogus-boo,
What can he do
But huffle in the dark?
So don't take fright;
He has no bite
And very little bark.

James Reeves

The Wendigo

The Wendigo,
The Wendigo!
Its eyes are ice and indigo!
Its blood is rank and yellowish!
Its voice is hoarse and bellowish!
Its tentacles are slithery,
And scummy,
Slimy,
Leathery!
Its lips are hungry blubbery,
And smacky,
Sucky,
Rubbery!

The Wendigo,
The Wendigo!
I saw it just a friend ago!
Last night it lurked in Canada;
Tonight, on your veranada!
As you are lolling hammockwise
It contemplates you stomachwise.
You loll,
It contemplates,
It lollops.
The rest is merely gulps and gollops.

Ogden Nash

Loach

The best pet I ever had
was a fish I caught in a net.
It was three inches long
and it had six whiskers round its mouth.
I looked it up in a book
and they said it was called a loach,
not roach — loach.

I put it in a tank
but the tank was by the window
where the sun came in,
so the tank went green,
a very very dark green.
And no one believed
I had anything in there —
let alone anything called a loach.
They said: 'All you've got in there
is snails and old pond-weed.'

Sometimes I'd go and sit by the tank,
and look in.
And I wouldn't see anything at all.
But sometimes I'd go and sit by the tank
and my loach would suddenly
come to the wall of the tank
where I could see it,
and I'd watch it
push the glass wall
push its whiskers along the gravel on the bottom
and then go back into the dark green water
where I couldn't see it, any more.

But no one believed I had anything in there
because no one ever sat by the tank
long enough to see it.

Michael Rosen

The Shark

He seemed to know the harbour,
So leisurely he swam;
His fin,
Like a piece of sheet-iron,
Three-cornered,
And with knife-edge,
Stirred not a bubble
As it moved
With its base-line on the water.

His body was tubular
And tapered
And smoke-blue,
And as he passed the wharf
He turned,
And snapped at a flat-fish
That was dead and floating.
And I saw the flash of a white throat,
And a double row of white teeth,
And eyes of metallic grey,
Hard and narrow and slit.

Then out of the harbour,
With that three-cornered fin,
Shearing without a bubble the water
Lithely,
Leisurely,
He swam —
That strange fish,
Tubular, tapered, smoke-blue,
Part vulture, part wolf,
Part neither — for his blood was cold.

E. J. Pratt

Seal

See how he dives
From rocks with a zoom!
See how he darts
Through his watery room
Past crabs and eels
And green seaweed,
Past fluffs of sandy
Minnow feed!
See how he swims
With a swerve and a twist,
A flip of the flipper,
A flick of the wrist!
Quicksilver-quick,
Softer than spray,
Down he plunges
And sweeps away;
Before you can think,
Before you can utter
Words like 'Dill pickle'
Or 'Apple butter',
Back up he swims
Past sting-ray and shark,
Out with a zoom,
A whoop, a bark;
Before you can say
Whatever you wish,
He plops at your side
With a mouthful of fish!

William Jay Smith

Gums

Gums is our fish at school,
We have birds and gerbils too.
I think Gums is the best.
We named him Gums
Because he had no teeth,
He swims around his home like a shark,
Guarding all his valuable things.

Andrew McDuff

below the falls
a leaping trout   scatters
the morning mist

John Wills

Whales

All the whales in the wider deeps, hot are they, as they urge
on and on, and dive beneath the icebergs.
The right whales, the sperm-whales, the hammer-heads,
    the killers
there they blow, there they blow, hot wild white breath out
    of the sea!

D. H. Lawrence

The Littleton Whale

In memory of Charles Olson

This poem is in the form of a letter from Charles Tomlinson of Gloucestershire, England, to Charles Olson of Gloucestershire, Massachusetts, who had written to ask for information about the River Severn.

What you wrote to know
was whether
the old ship canal
still paralleled the river
south
of Gloucester (England) ...

What I never told
in my reply
was of the morning
on that same stretch
(it was a cold
January day in '85)
when Isobel Durnell
saw the whale ...

She was up at dawn
to get her man off on time
to the brickyard and
humping over the banks
beyond Bunny Row
a slate-grey hill showed
that the night before
had not been there ...

They both ran outside
and down to the shore:
the wind was blowing
as it always blows
so hard that the tide
comes creeping up under it
often unheard ...

The great grey-blue thing
had an eye
that watched wearily
their miniature motions as they
debated its fate
for the tide
was already feeling beneath it
floating it away ...

It was Moses White
master mariner
owner of the sloop *Matilda*
who said the thing to do
was to get chains and a traction engine
— they got two from Olveston —
and drag it ashore:
the thing was a gift:
before long it would be
drifting off to another part of the coast
and lost to them
if they didn't move now ...

And so the whale —
flukes, flesh, tail
trembling no longer
with a failing life —
was chained and hauled
installed above the tideline ...

And the crowds came
to where it lay
upside down
displaying a
belly evenly-wrinkled
its eye lost to view
mouth skewed and opening into
an interior of tongue and giant sieves
that had once
filtered that diet of shrimp

its deep-sea sonar
had hunted out for it
by listening to submarine echoes
too slight
for electronic selection . . .

And Hector Knapp
wrote in his diary:
Thear was a whal
cum ashore at Littleton Pill
and bid thear a fortnight
He was sixty eaight feet long
His mouth was twelve feet
The Queen claim it at last
and sould it for forty pound
Thear supposed to be
forty thousen pepeal to see it
from all parts of the cuntry . . .

The Methodist preacher
said that George Sindry
who was a very religious man
told himself when that whale came in
he'd heard so many arguments
about the tale of Jonah not being true
that he went to Littleton to
'satisfy people'. He was a tall man
a six footer
'but I got into that whale's mouth' he said
'and I stood in it
upright . . .'

The carcass
had overstayed its welcome
so they sent up a sizeable boat
to tow it to Bristol
and put it on show there
before they cut the thing down stinking
to be sold
and spread for manure . . .

You can still see the sign
to Whale Wharf as they renamed it
and Wintle's Brickworks became
the Whale Brick
Tile and Pottery Works . . .

Walking daily onto
the now-gone premises
through the 'pasture land
with valuable deposits of clay underneath'
when the machine and drying sheds
the five kilns, the stores and stables
stood permanent in that place
of their disappearance

Enoch Durnell still
relished his part in all that history begun
when Bella shook
and woke him with a tale that the tide
had washed up a whole house
with blue slates on it into Littleton Pill
and that house was a whale . . .

Charles Tomlinson

Did you ever see an otter?
Silvery-sided, fish-fanged, fierce-faced, whiskered, mottled.

D. H. Lawrence

Little Fish

The tiny fish enjoy themselves
in the sea.
Quick little splinters of life,
their little lives are fun to them
in the sea.

D. H. Lawrence

The Guppy

Whales have calves,
Cats have kittens,
Bears have cubs,
Bats have bittens;
Swans have cygnets,
Seals have puppies,
But guppies just have little guppies.

Ogden Nash

A Visit to the Aquarium

Watching the conger eel

(a three foot slice of muscle,
a blue blade of steel
that cast a motionless shadow
on the lit glass floor of its cell)

I saw the sudden whiplash ripple
of its whole body
that crashed the plunging water
as it swallowed
and then was still

And I thought of my friend Dave Dirt,
too fast to live, too young to die,
who
sudden as lightning

    SWIPED

the Last Cake
at Phyllis Willis's birthday party!

Dave and the conger eel:
neither of them like to leave
anything to chance . . .
or to anyone
else.

Kit Wright

CONGER EEL

Barn Owl

Ernie Morgan found him, a small
Fur mitten inexplicably upright,
And hissing like a treble kettle
Beneath the tree he'd fallen from.
His bright eye frightened Ernie,
Who popped a rusty bucket over him
And ran for us. We kept him
In a backyard shed, perched
On the rung of a broken deck-chair,
Its canvas faded to his down's biscuit,
Men from the pits, their own childhood
Spent waste in the crippling earth,
Held him gently, brought him mice
From the wealth of our riddled tenements,
Saw that we understood his tenderness,
His tiny body under its puffed quilt,
Then left us alone. We called him Snowy.

He was never clumsy. He flew
From the first like a skilled moth,
Sifting the air with feathers.
Floating it softly to the place he wanted.
At dusk he'd stir, preen, stand
At the window-ledge, fly. It was
A catching of the heart to see him go.
Six months we kept him, saw him
Grow beautiful in a way each thought
His own knowledge. One afternoon, home
With pretended illness, I watched him
Leave. It was daylight. He lifted slowly
Over the Hughes's roof, his cream face calm,
And never came back. I saw this;
And tell it for the first time,
Having wanted to keep his mystery.

Leslie Norris   (an extract)

Lark

spi
nni
ng
at
the
 pe
ak
of
an
inv
isi
ble
je
t o
f w
ate
r,
you
 bu
rn
a b
lac
k s
tar
at
th
e h
ear
t o
f t
he
blu
e a
ppl
e w
e c
all
 sk
y,
LARK

George MacBeth

Disappearer
Re

Duck on the water.

He's gone!

Where?

Oh.

Diving duck.

comes again.

Here he

Robert Froman

Pigeons

They paddle with staccato feet
In powder-pools of sunlight,
Small blue busybodies
Strutting like fat gentlemen
With hands clasped
Under their swallowtail coats;
And, as they stump about,
Their heads like tiny hammers
Tap at imaginary nails
In non-existent walls.
Elusive ghosts of sunshine
Slither down the green gloss
Of their necks an instant, and are gone.

Summer hangs drugged from sky to earth
In limpid fathoms of silence:
Only warm dark dimples of sound
Slide like slow bubbles
From the contented throats.

Raise a casual hand —
With one quick gust
They fountain into air.

Richard Kell

Easy Diver

Pigeon on the roof.

Dives.

Go-

ing

fa-

st.

G
O
I
N
G

T
O

HIT HARD!

O p e n s   *w i n g s.*

Softly,   *gently,*

down.

Robert Froman

The Crow

By the wave rising, by the wave breaking
high to low;
by the wave riding the air, sweeping the high air low
in a white foam, in a suds,
there
like a church-warden, like a stiff
turn-the-eye-inward old man
in a cut-away, in the mist
stands
the crow.

P. K. Page

Spill

the wind scatters
a flock of sparrows —
a handful of small change
spilled suddenly
from the cloud's pocket.

Judith Thurman

Searching on the wind,
the hawk's cry . . .
is the shape of its beak.

J. W. Hackett

A bitter morning:
sparrows sitting together
without any necks.

J. W. Hackett

Parrot

I am proud.
My head is as green as an apple
And my voice is loud.
When I talk
It comes out in a marvellous squawk.
Everybody jumps.
I crack sweet nuts
And sit
Spitting shells and splitting pits.
When that gets dull
I tear paper into little bits.
Then I split and spit some more
And watch them rush to sweep the floor.
At night
All the funny people come to dinner
Dressed in jewels that clank and shiny leathers
To hide the fact that they do not have feathers.
They gabble, rattle, chitter, chatter
In mouse high squeaks
And low bear growls,
Speaking about something called 'war'
And someplace called 'Downtown'
And someone called 'Mrs.'
And what she wore the afternoon they met her.
People's talk sounds boring.
Parrots' talk sounds better.

Squawk

Karla Kuskin

The Toucan

Tell me who can
Catch a toucan?
Lou can.

Just how few can
Ride the toucan?
Two can.

What kind of goo can
Stick you to the toucan?
Glue can.

Who can write some
More about the toucan?
You can!

Shel Silverstein

Vulture

Veering and wheeling
high in the ceiling
of the Sahara sky
I can tell a bone
from a whitewashed stone
with my telescopic eye.

I look like a witch
flown up out of a ditch
dishevelled and dirty but never-
the-less horrifying,
for I eat the dying
and dead who are with me for ever.

My hooked beak is like
a scythe or a spike
for tearing the flesh from the skeleton.
My skin is as hoary
as the Old Hermit's story
or the filthy old paper they tell it on.

I love offal and scrag
or a bit of old rag
and for sweets I eat eyeballs of camels;
the most delicious
of edible dishes
for me is the dead flesh of mammals.

Vulture on high
I watch heroes die
as they fail to traverse the Sahara;
I drop like a wreath
on their bones underneath,
then I place their false teeth
on my bald head like a tiara.

George Barker

Death of a Mouse

A mouse returning late one night
Happy, or mildly drunk,
Danced a gavotte by the pale moonlight.
An owl caught sight of him.

Clunk.

James Fenton

A Dead Mole

Strong-shouldered mole,
That so much lived below the ground,
Dug, fought and loved, hunted and fed,
For you to raise a mound
Was as for us to make a hole;
What wonder now that being dead
Your body lies here stout and square
Buried within the blue vault of the air?

Andrew Young

The Day Our Dog Died

It was Sunday morning when I awoke
To see the face of my mum.
She, her eyes full of tears, said
Softly, unsteadily, 'She ... She's
Gone in her sleep.'
I felt upset, yet in a way
Happy —
For she was blind and almost deaf
But full of life.
It seemed a cruel kind of thing,
Like one of the family had died.
I waited until my mum had gone,
And for a while cried.
I went downstairs, my head aching
And my dog gone.

Ramona Harris

Fledgling

Yesterday in the early evening
some starlings dropped a fledgling,
hurled it rather, in at the garage door.
It fell face down and lay
spread on the concrete, wet and moving.
I stood for a while hoping that it would die,
that nothing would be demanded of me
except to throw it away.
Its neck was stretched like a bird flying,
and the wings twitched. Suddenly
as I watched, both its legs
strained, the claws scoured the floor
desperate, urgent; yet all the time
the blind head, separate, did not move.

I dug a hole in the bed
where last year we had geraniums,
and for some reason gently, laid it
on the damp soil. For the first time then
the head moved; the beak opened
in a great silent cry of protest,
then closed, then opened again
huge like a yawn, yellow, exaggerated,
crying out soundlessly for pity

which was the spade's edge falling.

Jim Howell

The sack of kittens

The sack of kittens
sinking in the icy creek,
increases the cold.

Nicholas Virgilio

The Mole

The mole (it may have been vole: I can't distinguish)
Lay by the roadside and squeaked out his fear
While two big dogs drew off as I drew near.
He squeaked and thrust and thrust his head in anguish
Telling his pain and grief in a mole's language
And tried a refuge in the earth to tear
Knowing his safety nowhere else but there,
There where the small hands strove to win advantage.

For that's the best-laid scheme of moles and men,
To get down under in the healing gloom,
Calm in the dark and soundless in the ground.
I lifted him to where he might begin
To shape a hiding-place, a gentle room,
A simple dwelling and a humble mound.

Roy Daniells

Rats

Rats, they're terrible things,
We cut one up in school today.
First the intestines — they were slimy,
She cut them out.
Then the kidneys ...
I looked away.
When I looked back, there was an assortment,
A heart, his tail
And other things.
It looked horrible,
Just like a bad dream.
A bad smell came up
I rushed to the window —
Soon the rat was empty,
The pieces were out in the tin.

Jimmy Went

The Stag

While the rain fell on the November woodland shoulder of
      Exmoor
While the traffic jam along the road honked and shouted
Because the farmers were parking wherever they could
And scrambling to the bank-top to stare through the tree-fringe
Which was leafless,
The stag ran through his private forest.

While the rain drummed on the roofs of the parked cars
And the kids inside cried and daubed their chocolate and fought
And mothers and aunts and grandmothers
Were a tangle of undoing sandwiches and screwed-round
      gossiping heads
Steaming up the windows,
The stag loped through his favourite valley.

While the blue horsemen down in the boggy meadow
Sodden nearly black, on sodden horses,
Spaced as at a military parade,
Moved a few paces to the right and a few to the left and felt
      rather foolish
Looking at the brown impassable river,
The stag came over the last hill of Exmoor.

While everybody high-kneed it to the bank-top all along
      the road
Where steady men in oilskins were stationed at binoculars,
And the horsemen by the river galloped anxiously this way
      and that
And the cry of hounds came tumbling invisibly with their
      echoes down through the draggle of trees,
Swinging across the wall of dark woodland,
The stag dropped into a strange country.

And turned at the river
Hearing the hound-pack smash the undergrowth, hearing
      the bell-note
Of the voice that carried all the others,
Then while his limbs all cried different directions to his
      lungs, which only wanted to rest,
The blue horsemen on the bank opposite
Pulled aside the camouflage of their terrible planet.

And the stag doubled back weeping and looking for home
      up a valley and down a valley
While the strange trees struck at him and the brambles
      lashed him,
And the strange earth came galloping after him carrying
      the loll-tongued hounds to fling all over him
And his heart became just a club beating his ribs and his
      own hooves shouted with hounds' voices,
And the crowd on the road got back into their cars
Wet-through and disappointed.

Ted Hughes

'We are going to see the Rabbit'

We are going to see the rabbit,
We are going to see the rabbit.
Which rabbit, people say?
Which rabbit, ask the children?
Which rabbit?
The only rabbit,
The only rabbit in England,
Sitting behind a barbed-wire fence
Under the floodlights, neon lights,
Sodium lights,
Nibbling grass
On the only patch of grass
In England, in England
(Except the grass by the hoardings
Which doesn't count.)
We are going to see the rabbit
And we must be there on time.
First we shall go by escalator,
Then we shall go by underground,
And then we shall go by motorway
And then by helicopterway,
And the last ten yards we shall have to go
On foot.

And now we are going
All the way to see the rabbit,
We are nearly there,
We are longing to see it,
And so is the crowd
Which is here in thousands
With mounted policemen
And big loudspeakers
And bands and banners,
And everyone has come a long way.
But soon we shall see it

Sitting and nibbling
The blades of grass
On the only patch of grass
In — but something has gone wrong!
Why is everyone so angry
Why is everyone jostling
And slanging and complaining?

The rabbit has gone,
Yes, the rabbit has gone.
He has actually burrowed down into the earth
And made himself a warren, under the earth,
Despite all these people.
And what shall we do?
What *can* we do?

It is all a pity, you must be disappointed,
Go home and do something else for today,
Go home again, go home for today.
For you cannot hear the rabbit, under the earth,
Remarking rather sadly to himself, by himself,
As he rests in his warren, under the earth:
'It won't be long, they are bound to come,
They are bound to come and find me, even here.'

Alan Brownjohn

The Mad Yak

I am watching them churn the last milk they'll ever get
    from me.
They are waiting for me to die;
They want to make buttons out of my bones.
Where are my sisters and brothers?
That tall monk there, loading my uncle, he has a new cap.
And that idiot student of his — I never saw that muffler
    before.
Poor uncle, he lets them load him.
How sad he is, how tired!
I wonder what they'll do with his bones?
And that beautiful tail!
How many shoelaces will they make of that!

Gregory Corso

118

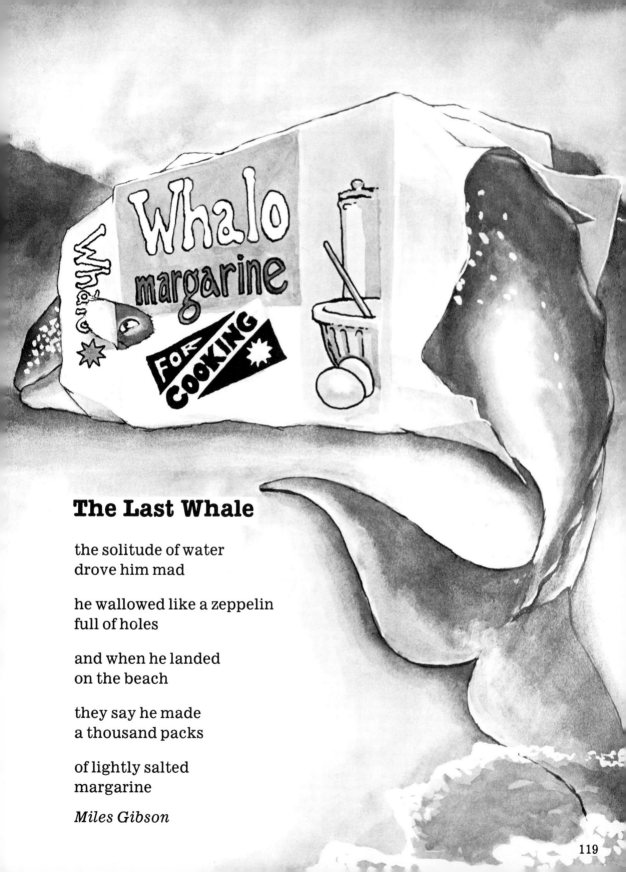

The Last Whale

the solitude of water
drove him mad

he wallowed like a zeppelin
full of holes

and when he landed
on the beach

they say he made
a thousand packs

of lightly salted
margarine

Miles Gibson

Buffalo Dusk

The buffaloes are gone.
And those who saw the buffaloes are gone.
Those who saw the buffaloes by thousands and
    how they pawed the prairie sod into dust
    with their hoofs, their great heads down
    pawing on in a great pageant of dusk,
Those who saw the buffaloes are gone.
And the buffaloes are gone.

Carl Sandburg

Complaint of the Wild Goose

We were nine to leave the lake in the north;
Of the nine travellers, I am the last.
Noble hunting falcon, have pity on me.

My country is far; the winds are contrary;
My wings grown heavy, I followed behind, alone.
Noble hunting falcon, have pity on me.

The leaders are at the nest, the stragglers are passing the
    halting-place;
Winter is coming, the sky is clouded.
Noble hunting falcon, have pity on me.

The sky is gray, the winds rise;
I hear my brothers flying on through the fog.
Noble hunting falcon, have pity on me.

Western Mongolian lullaby

The Great Auk's Ghost

The Great Auk's ghost rose on one leg,
Sighed thrice and three times winkt,
And turned and poached a phantom egg
And muttered, 'I'm extinct.'

Ralph Hodgson

Index of Titles and First Lines

Acknowledgements

The editor and publisher would like to thank the following for permission to reprint copyright poems. Every effort has been made to trace and contact copyright holders but this has not always been possible. If we have inadvertently omitted to acknowledge anyone we should be grateful if this could be brought to our attention for correction at the first opportunity.

Conrad Aiken: 'Elephantelope' from *Who's Zoo* (illustrated by John Vernon Lord). Reprinted by permission of Jonathan Cape Ltd. **Michael Baldwin**: 'The Small Brown Bear' was first published in *A First Poetry Book* (OUP, 1979). **George Barker**: extract from 'Vulture', extract from 'Puma' and extract from 'Yeti, the Abominable Snowman' from *The Alphabetical Zoo*. Reprinted by permission of Faber & Faber Ltd. **Keith Bosley**: 'Egg O Egg...', 'Cat purring...' and 'Snake glides...' from *And I Dance*. Reprinted by permission of Angus & Robertson (UK) Ltd. **Geoffrey Bownas and Anthony Thwaite**: 'Disturbed, the cat...' (Modern Senryu) from *The Penguin Book of Japanese Verse*, trans. Geoffrey Bownas & Anthony Thwaite (Penguin Poets, 1964). Copyright © Geoffrey Bownas and Anthony Thwaite. Reprinted by permission of Penguin Books Ltd. **Alan Brownjohn**: 'Horse', 'Leopard' and 'Monkey' from *Brownjohn's Beasts*. 'We're going to see the rabbit' first published in *The Railings* (Digby Press). All reprinted by permission of Macmillan, London and Basingstoke. **Sheelagh Carville**: 'The Frog' from *The Scrake of Dawn*: Poems by young people from Northern Ireland (ed. Paul Muldoon). Reprinted by permission of Blackstaff Press Ltd. **Leonard Clark**: 'Bear' from *The Broad Atlantic*. Reprinted by permission of Dennis Dobson Publishers. **Sue Cochrane**: 'Slide-Swim-Fly' from *Big Dipper*. Reprinted by permission of Oxford University Press, Melbourne. **Gregory Corso**: 'The Mad Yak' from *Long Live Man*. Copyright © 1959, 1960, 1961, 1962 by New Directions Publishing Corp. Reprinted by permission. **Darren Coyles**: 'Cheetah' was first published in *Children as Writers: 21st year: W.H. Smith*. Reprinted by permission of Heinemann Educational Books. **Roy Daniells**: 'The Mole' from *Deeper Into the Forest*. Reprinted by permission of the Canadian Publishers, McClelland and Stewart Ltd., Toronto. **Fiona Davison**: 'The Slabbery Fingers' from *Under the Moon, Over the Stars* (ed. Michael Longley). Reprinted by permission of the Arts Council of Northern Ireland. **Francis Edwards**: 'Dragon Poem' from *Hey Mister Butterfly* (ed. Alasdair Aston, ILEA). By permission. **D.J. Enright**: 'Better be kind to them now' from *Rhyme Times Rhyme* (Chatto & Windus). Copyright © 1974 D.J. Enright. Reprinted by permission of Bolt & Watson Ltd., author's agent. **James Fenton**: 'Death of a mouse'. Reprinted by permission of the author. **Rachel Fewster**: 'Poem to Spiders' from *See What I Say*. Reprinted by permission of Oxford University Press, Melbourne. **Robert Froman**: 'Easy Diver' and 'Dis/Re-Appeared' from *Seeing Things*. Reprinted by permission of Abelard-Schuman Ltd. (Blackie Publ. Group). **Miles Gibson**: 'The Last Whale' *The Guilty Bystander* (Methuen Children's Books). Reprinted by permission of Associated Book Publishers Ltd. **Gail Gregory**: 'Farmyard' from *Big Dipper*. Reprinted by permission of Oxford University Press, Melbourne. **J.W. Hackett**: 'A bitter morning...', 'Searching on the wind,...' from *The Way of Haiku* (A volume of original haiku) by J.W. Hackett, published by Japan Publications, Inc., Tokyo, © 1968. Reprinted by permission of the author. **Ramona Harris**: 'The Day our Dog Died' from *Stepney Words 1 & 2*. Reprinted by permission of Centerprise Trust Ltd. **Phoebe Hesketh**: 'Old Horse' from *A Song of Sunlight*. Reprinted by permission of Chatto & Windus Ltd., for the author. **Ralph Hodgson**: 'The Great Auk's Ghost' from *Collected Poems*. Reprinted by permission of Mrs. Hodgson and Macmillan, London and Basingstoke. **Russell Hoban**: 'Small, smaller' from *The Pedalling Man* text copyright © 1968 by Russell Hoban. Published in the UK and British Commonwealth by World's Work Ltd., and in Canada by Grosset & Dunlap Inc. Reprinted by permission of the publishers. **Hugh Hodge**: 'A Guinea-pig' was first published in *Children as Writers: 21st Year: W.H. Smith*. Reprinted by permission of Heinemann Educational Books. **Jim Howell**: 'Fledgling' from *Survivals* (Harry Chambers/Peterloo Poets, 1976). By permission. **Ted Hughes**: 'Nessie' from *Moon Bells and Other Poems* (published by Chatto & Windus). 'The Stag' from *Season Songs*. 'The Thought Fox' from *Hawk in the Rain* (Faber) and also in *Selected Poems*. Copyright © 1957 by Ted Hughes, originally appeared in *The New Yorker*. Reprinted by permission of Faber & Faber Ltd., and of Harper & Row, Publishers, Inc. **James Hurley**: 'Greedy Dog'. Reprinted by permission of the author. **David Jackson**: 'Catching Butterflies'. Reprinted by permission of the author. **Richard Kell**: 'Pigeons' from *Differences*. Reprinted by permission of Chatto & Windus Ltd., for the author. **Mohammed Khan**: 'I have this crazy problem'. **Roger Kilroy** (ed.): 'Beware of the Dog' from *Graffiti: The Scrawl of the Wild*, edited by Roger Kilroy. Reprinted by permission of Transworld Publishers Ltd. (Corgi Books). **Raymond Knister**: 'White Cat' from *The Collected Poems of Raymond Knister*. Copyright 1949. Reprinted by permission of McGraw-Hill Ryerson Ltd., Toronto. **Karla Kuskin**: Poem no.22 'I am Proud...', Poem no.2 'I do not understand...', Poem no.4 'If, you...' from *Any Me I Want to Be*. Copyright © 1972 by Karla Kuskin. Reprinted by permission of Harper & Row, Publishers, Inc. **Stewart Lackie**: 'The Dinosaur' from *Hey Mister Butterfly* (edited by Alasdair Aston, ILEA). By permission. **Anne LeRoy**: 'In the bush' from *Big Dipper*. Reprinted by permission of Oxford University Press, Melbourne. **John Mbiti**: 'The Snake Song'. Reprinted by permission of the author. **Oswald Mbuyiseni Mtshali**: 'A Newly-born Calf' from *Sounds of a Cowhide Drum*. Copyright © Oswald Joseph Mtshali 1971. Reprinted by permission of Oxford University Press. **George MacBeth**: 'Lark'. Reprinted by permission of the author. **Carson McCullers**: 'Giraffe' from *Sweet as a Pickle and Clean as a Pig*. Copyright © 1962 by Carson McCullers and Rolf Gerard. Reprinted by permission of Jonathan Cape Ltd., and of Houghton Mifflin Company. **Andrew McDuff**: 'Gums' from *The Scrake of Dawn*. Poems by young people from Northern Ireland (ed. Paul Muldoon). Reprinted by permission of Blackstaff Press Ltd. **Edwin Morgan**: 'Hyena' from *From Glasgow to Saturn* (Carcanet